Comparing Past and Present

Going on a Trip

Rebecca Rissman

Raintree is an imprint of Capstone Global Library Limited, a company incorporated in England and Wales having its registered office at 7 Pilgrim Street, London, EC4V 6LB – Registered company number: 6695582

www.raintreepublishers.co.uk
myorders@raintreepublishers.co.uk

Text © Capstone Global Library Limited 2014
First published in hardback in 2014
The moral rights of the proprietor have been asserted.

Edited by Rebecca Rissman, Daniel Nunn, and Catherine Veitch
Designed by Philippa Jenkins
Picture research by Elizabeth Alexander
Production by Helen McCreath
Originated by Capstone Global Library Ltd
Printed and bound in China

ISBN 978 1 4062 7150 8
17 16 15 14 13
10 9 8 7 6 5 4 3 2 1

British Library Cataloguing in Publication Data
A full catalogue record for this book is available from the British Library.

Acknowledgements

We would like to thank the following for permission to reproduce photographs: © Capstone Publishers p. 5 (Karon Dubke); Alamy pp. 6 (© ClassicStock), 12 (© Vintage Images), 13 (© Juice Images), 20 (© Archive Pics), 22 (© INTERFOTO); Corbis pp. 4 (© H. Armstrong Roberts), 15 (© Redlink Production), 23 (© Redlink Production); Getty Images pp. 8 (Hulton Archive/Topical Press Agency), 18 (Hulton Archive/Sasha), 21 (Gallo Images/Danita Delimont); Shutterstock pp. 7 (© Pavel L Photo and Video), 11 (© cynoclub), 17 (© Pavel L Photo and Video), SuperStock pp. 9 (Alex Mares-Manton/Asia Images), 10, 14, 16 (Universal Images Group), 19, 23.

Front cover photographs of a young couple enjoying a car ride, 1907, reproduced with permission of Superstock (Everett Collection), and a family loading inflatables into a car reproduced with permission of Getty Images (Image Source). Back cover photograph of people in a horse-drawn carriage, New Hampshire, USA reproduced with permission of Superstock.

We would like to thank Nancy Harris and Diana Bentley for their invaluable help in the preparation of this book.

Every effort has been made to contact copyright holders of material reproduced in this book. Any omissions will be rectified in subsequent printings if notice is given to the publisher.

Contents

Comparing the past and present

Things in the past have already happened.

Things in the present are happening now.

Travelling has changed over time.

The way people take trips in the present is very different to the past.

Getting around

In the past most people walked
from place to place.

Today, many people only walk
a short way.

In the past many people used horses to travel.

Today, some people ride horses for fun.

In the past few people took trips
in cars.

Today, many people take trips
in cars.

In the past people travelled across oceans in large ships.

Today, people can travel across oceans in aeroplanes.

Who travels?

In the past only rich families went on long trips.

Today, many families go on
long trips.

How long did it take?

In the past it could take weeks to travel to a new place.

Today, people can travel around
the world in just hours.

Why travel?

In the past some people travelled far away to start a new life.

Today, people also travel for work and
to see new places.

Then and now

In the past people went on trips for fun.
Today, people still go on trips for fun!

Picture glossary

 **aeroplane** large machine that flies through the air

 **ship** large boat that carries many people a long way

Index

Notes for parents and teachers

Before reading

Talk to children about the difference between the past and present. Explain that things that have already happened are in the past. Remind children of a classroom activity that took place a day or two ago, and explain how that activity happened in the past. Then explain that the conversation you are having now is in the present.

After reading

- Explain to children that the way people travel has changed over time. Ask children to think of different modes of transport, such as car, bicycle, aeroplane, or train. Then explain that some of these modes of transport did not exist in the past.

- Tell children that the word *hoilday* means a special trip people take to enjoy themselves. Ask children if they have ever taken a hoilday. If so, ask them to explain where they went, how they got there, and how long the trip took. Then, as a group, brainstorm about how the trip might have been different if it had taken place in the past.

- Ask children if they have ever seen or rode a horse. Explain that in the past, many people used horses for transport. Show children the photo on page 10. Ask if they think travelling by horse would have been fast or slow.